*For Lindsay, Brittany, and our beloved Babs.
My travel companions on this journey.*

Acknowledging My Tribe

After tragedy strikes, reality looms, and everyone goes home to resume their lives, you learn who your tribe is. The people that stay. Feed you. Sit with you in silence. Let you cry, or laugh, without judgment. Understand what you've lost. Remind you of who you are. Celebrate your victories. Keep these people close.

Thank you...

To Jeff, my best friend and the love of my life for 23 years. For being an honest, gentle, hardworking, loving husband and friend and an outstanding role model for our daughters. You are still a part of everything we do.

To Lindsay and Brittany, the two best things I've done with my life. You amaze me with your strength, resilience, humor and positively foul language. Our laughter has gotten us through so very much and you are the brightest stars in my universe.

To Mary. You are one of the finest people I've ever known. Thank you for sharing your son, and yourself with our family; for your ongoing love, support and encouragement. You have never wavered.

Finally, to Brad. For seeing my potential in the broken pieces. You taught me to smile again when I was at my lowest. You took on my girls and have loved and encouraged them as your own – even when they didn't make it easy. You have encouraged memories of Jeff to remain a positive influence in our lives. It takes a strong man with a generous heart to be "Plan B" and you are my biggest supporter. Thank you for being my rock and the love of the second half of my life.

Introduction

I don't have a college degree, impressive credentials following my name or framed plaques gracing my walls. I don't know a lot about many things, but I do know a bit about some things and a lot about one thing. Loss. I'm not a writer, but I have a story to tell.

Nothing anyone could have done or said could have prepared me for the uncharted journey that has led me to where I stand today in tattered boots. As I survey the surrounding landscape, reflect on the numerous roadblocks and wrong turns I've taken along the way, I am abundantly grateful. It didn't happen overnight, believe me. I've been full of rage, depressed, exhausted, worried, sad, and pretty much run the gamut of emotions that appear online when you Google "bereaved." It's a solitary journey that covers new and sometimes hostile territory and requires fortitude, grit and sturdy shoes. There is no backpack of soul food, healing tools, navigational instruments or terrain maps. I am metaphorically referring to that five letter word called "GRIEF" and the ongoing process of seeking and cultivating peace, purpose and beauty when your life is "FUBAR" (another five-letter word.)

Aside from birth and death (and some would argue taxes), grief is perhaps one of the few things every human being will experience at some time in their life. Of course, the emotions brought about by grief are expressed uniquely by individual based on cultural, religious, and social norms but the overarching experience is one of intense emotional and often physical pain. They don't call it heartache for nothing. A broken heart is uncomfortable and might beat to an odd rhythm that makes normal breathing difficult. Often, grief stems from the death of a friend or loved one but can also be the result of the loss of a pet, a new diagnosis or chronic illness, divorce, loss of employment and many other events, all of which are complicated, difficult and downright messy.

As a mother, I know the pain, guilt and fear I experienced when my 11-month old daughter, in a coma and near death, was subsequently diagnosed with Type 1 Diabetes. At that time, she was the youngest person ever diagnosed in the State of Washington.

I know the sadness of losing my dad to a vicious disease of unknown etiology at the age of 69.

I know the angst caused by unexpected job loss.

I know the emotional toll that occurs when someone you love is the victim of a violent crime.

And I know the life altering trauma of the sudden death of a spouse.

I've sprinkled the cremated remains of the man I loved under our apple tree, on Mount Haleakala in Maui and, yes, on my tongue.

With the death of a partner, it's not only the loss of your "person" and the life you created together, it's the end of the future you dreamed of and thought you had. It's the end of security and comfort. The end of normal. The end of "us."

Growing up, death was never really addressed in my family. It certainly wasn't a taboo subject, but opportunities for open discussion were few and far between with the passing of an elderly neighbor or distant relative. As a young adult, the death of my grandparents was my first experience with loss and all that accompanies it. But they had both led long, healthy, rich lives and were, well...old. It wasn't completely out of the blue. It was difficult, but it made sense in the natural order of things. I've often wondered if loss feels different if you know it's coming. After a prolonged illness, does the death of a loved one hurt less? If you have the opportunity to share important sentiments before death, is guilt alleviated, or, is a sudden loss "better"? Pretty sure it all stinks. There's just no comfortable, tidy way to say a final goodbye to someone who has held space in your heart and life.

One minute life is good. And then it's not.

I know what shattering, searing, gut-wrenching, ass-kicking grief is. I didn't think I would survive. At times, I didn't want to. Yet every morning, my eyes would open to the new day.

I know about fear, brain fog, being faced with what used to be every time you come home from work, crying in the shower or the restroom at work, and the desperation that levels you when the one thing you want more than anything is the one thing that can never be. Where is the hope? How will I survive?

I know the bargaining. I would do anything to have him back again. Anything. I would do it twice.

This is not a book about the stages of grief with timelines and rules. I have read many of those, but they just didn't resonate with me, which made me feel even worse.

I'm here to encourage you to be gentle with yourself. There are no rules here. No judgment. Do what feels right, despite what others may think or feel is right. Let your tribe help in ways that truly help. Your body and soul are trying to make sense of the senseless – you may feel like you're losing your mind. You're not – there is no crazy here! It's OK to not be OK.

I, and so many others like you, understand some of what you may be feeling and you're not as alone as you think. You will come through the debilitating grief a changed person with a strength you never realized resided within. I'm fourteen years in and while I can still summon the pain, it usually just tiptoes beside me most days.

Everyone's journey through grief is individual and sacred, and I hope my story brings you moments of peace, clarity, and maybe even a chuckle.

Descent

What an amazing year 2005 was going to be! Full of milestones and long-anticipated achievements. I would turn 40 in November. My sister and I had plans to summit Mount Rainier. Jeff and I would celebrate our 20th wedding anniversary. Our daughter, Lindsay, would turn 18, graduate from high school, and begin higher education with plans to become a teacher. Brittany, our baby, would turn 16 and get behind the wheel of a car. We were an active family, with work to do, vacations to take, events to attend, friends to visit, and holiday plans to consider. Plans. We had lots of plans. Written on the calendar. In ink.

Before John Lennon was gunned down at the Dakota, he wrote "Life is what happens to you while you're busy making other plans." Robert Burns' poem *To a Mouse* reads, "The best laid plans of mice and men often go astray." Astray? What an understatement! In July and August of 2005, my idyllic life was hijacked, flown into the side of a mountain and left for dead.

It was September of 2004 and I was on the phone with my older, wiser sister, Terri, trying to persuade her to sign up for the July 2005 American Lung Association "Climb for Clean Air." It seemed the perfect marriage of wild adventure and a fitting tribute to our dad, who had passed away from pulmonary fibrosis in 1996 at the age of 69.

The climb is an annual fundraising event in the greater Seattle area. Accomplished climbers and novices alike (that's where Terri and I come in) individually raise significant pledges and spend the next several months preparing for the rigors of climbing the 14,411-foot beauty in a single attempt to reach the summit. The climb would begin at Paradise on Mount Rainier's south side. From there, we'd trek to Camp Muir at 10,000 feet. After food and a little rest, we'd be up between midnight, don headlamps and make a push for the summit via the Ingraham Glacier.

Terri was concerned that we didn't have enough time to adequately train, but I continued to manipulate as only a younger sister can. My fortieth birthday was fast approaching, and I was feeling the desire to do something outside my comfort zone. Push the boundaries. Stretch my wings. Climb a mountain. Mind you, I had never climbed anything more treacherous than my basement stairs in all my thirty-nine years! Still, it seemed a perfectly reasonable idea and I was determined that Terri's wings were also in need of a good stretch. With a bit more insistence I wore her down and she agreed to the challenge. Did I really say she was wiser?

There is nothing quite as awe-inspiring as Mount Rainier on a clear day in the Pacific Northwest. Her silhouette provides a stunning backdrop to the Seattle skyline and it's not uncommon to hear people comment "the mountain is out today." But for all her beauty and majesty, I now have a love-hate relationship with her.

The physical beauty Rainier National Park offers is second to none. The challenge of the climb was a tremendous learning experience and, for me, a once-in-a-lifetime opportunity. Sadly, I now associate Mt. Rainier with the beginning of the end of life as I knew it. The fork representing before and after. I know it sounds ridiculous to be angry at a mountain but, fork that bitch!

Suffice it to say, the ten months leading up to the climb were filled with preparation, planning meetings, many training hikes and daily grueling workouts. Terri and I were both very fortunate to have a great support system in our family, friends and co-workers and we both raised the required pledges with relative ease. Jeff, normally a private person, was overwhelmingly supportive of the endeavor and posted our blog updates and related news articles for his co-workers to follow. I was pleased with his interest and wanted to make him proud. Before we knew it, all the event hurdles had not only been met, but exceeded. Holy cow, we were really going to do this!

One of the many things I was able to take away from attempting the climb is how wonderful it is for likeminded people to tackle a common goal and learn to work together as a fluid team. We met so many amazing, courageous individuals, all with stories of their own and reasons precious to them for taking on such a challenge.

In close proximity, you also learn about individual temperaments, values, strengths and weaknesses. I also learned a few things about myself. Primarily, that I have a pretty low threshold for discomfort. When you're cold, tired and sore and still have hours of tough progress to make while focusing on the person's boots in front of you, it is easy to think, "What the heck am I doing here? I absolutely do not have to prove anything to anybody. It's ok to stop at any time. If a single person says anything about me stopping to rest, I will mercilessly impale them with my ice axe!" The difficult part can be shutting out that nagging self-doubt and negative thinking, finding your pace and continuing forward. Gradually, we all began to learn what parts of the climb were difficult for each other and tried to keep the focus on encouragement and positive reinforcement. Some of my happiest days were shared with Terri and our newfound friends on that mountain.

As the July 2005 climb date approached, Jeff and Brittany made plans to travel to the mountain with me. While I was off on my adventure, they would spend three days hiking and taking photos of the surrounding Park until I returned to Paradise Lodge. With the rare opportunity of having the house to herself, Lindsay opted to stay at home (can you say party?)

The night before the climb was spent relaxing at Whittaker's Bunkhouse in Ashford, Washington, at the base of Rainier, with none other than Lou Whittaker! Lou is a world-renowned mountaineer and glacier-travel guide. He and his twin brother, Jim, were born and raised in Seattle and Lou became the most experienced guide for climbing Mount Rainier. He also led the first American ascent of Mount Everest in 1984. The mood was light and there was an underlying feeling of excitement for what the coming days held. Lou shared stories, gave advice and told a few raunchy jokes. It was a warm sunny evening. Everyone was feeling good. Teams turned in early with packs and equipment ready to go.

Morning came very early with a hearty bite, equipment checks, more instructions and a van ride from the bunkhouse to Paradise, the hike to Alta Vista trailhead and the beginning of the climb. This was really it! No turning back now!

The weather was overcast with heavy drizzle and a light breeze as we headed up the steep path to the trailhead. There were six climbers on the team and two gregarious guides from Rainier Mountaineering, JJ and Mike. Several other teams had started their ascent the previous day and more would make the attempt in the days following.

The plan (there's that word again!) was to set a steady pace for base camp at Camp Muir, which sits between the Muir snowfield and the Cowlitz Glacier at an elevation of 10,080 feet. On arrival at base camp, it's critical to eat and rehydrate to ward off altitude sickness and grab whatever rest you can. The combination of too many bodies packed into a ramshackle building, damp clothes, body odors, unique personalities and lots of snoring can make it difficult to get truly restful sleep.

In the very early morning hours, when you've just managed to fall asleep, the guides roust everyone out of bed and, while it's still dark, usually around 1:00 am, the team puts on crampons, headlamps and ropes up for the final summit push. This is the safest time to approach the summit as the summer months have already opened crevasses and other dangers. It's best to head out before the sun hits the glacier. A few photo opportunities and celebratory moments will be spent at the summit before the descent begins.

The early stages of the climb were uneventful and unfolded as expected. The weather conditions added to the level of difficulty we were experiencing, and it was near whiteout conditions in some places. After several hours, we stopped to adjust gear and clothing for the increasing storm and continued. It was at that point that I began having nagging moments of self-doubt. As the wind began to howl, kick-stepping up 90-degree inclines made my legs feel weak and next steps unsteady.

What was I thinking? I had no business being on this mountain. Why did I think this was even remotely possible? I wanted to hurl myself down and cry. Just throw my head back like Charlie Brown and wail. Terri sensed my doubt and encouraged me to work through it. This cycle continued occasionally as we slowly gained altitude. Call it perseverance or sibling rivalry (probably the latter), but I didn't want to be a quitter. I talked Terri into this adventure, and I had too much pride not to finish.

Mike and JJ made frequent contact with the guides above us at base camp and those below at Paradise to gauge what kind of weather we were climbing into. We didn't realize that they were considering whether to continue to Muir or call it quits and return to the lodge.

The downpour at lower altitudes had turned to ice at our elevation and the wind, clocked at 70 miles per hour was pelting us, even knocking over one of the smaller women on the team. On the way up, the flow of water at Pebble Creek was at a standstill and looked as if it was blowing uphill in several places. I have never witnessed weather like this before. It was both amazing and a bit frightening. Before reaching base camp, a place we'd reached several times on training hikes, the guides decided the conditions were too dangerous to continue and turned the climb back toward the lodge.

What? How could this be happening? We had trained so long and hard and done everything right! This was our one and only shot and we were turning back before reaching Camp Muir? This wasn't fair! After several protests and arguments by all, the dejected team turned and began the descent. Ice and winds continued beating on us as we headed down the mountain. JJ and Mike, trying to keep spirits up, would whoop and shriek as they fell into the wind with all their weight and were pushed upright again.

As we descended out of the storm, the guides expressed how difficult it is to make the decision to "turn" a group when they know how many hope to realize a summit goal. They reminded us that safety is always their first priority. Even the most accomplished climbers can get into trouble quickly if they make even the slightest error in judgment. The mountain isn't going anywhere and while she won the game that day, we might win another day. I knew at that time there would be no other day for me. There was a small part of me that felt strangely relieved. The part that said I would never have summited anyway. Even so, I couldn't help but feel overwhelming disappointment.

Because our group was back sooner than expected, Paradise Lodge put us up for the night. Terri and I dropped off our gear in the room, changed into some dry clothes and promptly hit the bar. The next several hours were spent with other disappointed climbers, laughing and grousing about our individual experiences. Many were already looking toward upcoming climbs and for a few, this had been a training climb for Kilimanjaro. Terri and I weren't alone in our disappointment and we talked through much of our frustration that night. There were also plenty of laughs which lifted the mood. The alcohol may have played a part in that as well.

Jeff and Brittany cut their trip short and joined us at the Lodge. They had enjoyed their brief time hiking together and were happy to have me back down on solid ground. Rainier Mountaineering hosts a wonderful celebratory dinner for climbers and their families at the Lodge. The food was delicious, and the ambience was warm and inviting. The perfect way to end our great adventure before returning to our real lives! We learned later that the groups both ahead and behind ours had summited. We were the only group turned. The storm subsided almost as quickly as it had arrived, and the weather was beautiful once again. We decided to leave the following morning and would return home two days before we had originally planned.

That's the thing about plans.

Shot

Once home, I deposited my gear inside the front door, made a few calls to catch people up on what had happened, and promptly planted myself on the couch for a late afternoon nap. Ah, the comforts of home and family. After a bite of dinner, we plugged in a movie and settled in for a relaxing night. Brittany was on the computer in the family room and Lindsay had gone out for burgers with friends. The movie ended and I decided to take a hot shower and turn in. I was surprisingly exhausted and looking forward to sleeping in my own bed. Sweet slumber was only moments away! Or so I thought.

I was enjoying the steaming water and replaying the climb in my head when I heard a ruckus outside the bathroom. Suddenly, Jeff burst into the room and threw open the shower door. He had a wild look in his eyes that I'd never seen and all I could do was look at him as he stuttered "Lindsay just called me from I-5. She doesn't know what happened but thinks they may have been shot a couple of times while driving. They called 911 and are on the shoulder waiting. I'm going to go see if I can find them. I'll call you as soon as I know something." And then he was gone. I stood there covered in suds and tried to make sense of what he had just said.

Shot? With a gun? What the hell is going on? Who is she with? Lindsay, her best friend Erin and two guy friends,

Pat and Josh, were just going to get something to eat. What had she REALLY been up to? My brain was quickly spiraling down the rabbit hole as I quickly dried and dressed and met Brittany in the hall.

No more than ten minutes had passed when the phone rang. I answered immediately and heard Jeff's breathless voice say "I found her and she's ok, but she fucking got shot. Twice! Erin's been hit too and they're both being taken to Harborview. I'll be home in a few minutes to get you and Britt." I hung up and immediately lost it. People in this neighborhood don't get shot. Certainly not 17- year old socialites on the way to grab a burger. Do they? Brittany and I collected our things and went outside into the warm evening air, enveloped in each other's comforting arms, and waited for Jeff to arrive.

Moments later, Jeff pulled up, we jumped into the car and were off again. Ironically as we merged onto southbound I-5 toward downtown Seattle and Harborview Medical Center, we were sucked into a traffic jam of epic proportions and were moving at a snail's pace. It took several minutes before we realized that the shooting had caused this very backup!

Lindsay's car had been pulled off to the side of the freeway and one lane had been completely shut down as the police conducted their investigation. As we approached the scene, Jeff cautioned us that the car looked pretty bad. I thought I had braced myself but as we drove alongside the little silver Jetta with the Hawaiian print seat covers, there were four bullet holes torn in the side of the car. Police investigators, flashing lights, crime tape and news vehicles added to the horrific scene and both Brittany and I began crying in unison.

How could this be happening to Lindsay? To our family? And what, exactly HAD happened?

As we made our way through the sea of red lights, Jeff explained what little he knew of the situation. After Lindsay had called, Jeff had headed southbound on I-5 and before long saw two ambulances and a caravan of cars pulled over on the shoulder, and he knew he'd found them. He ran to the first ambulance and opened the door to see Erin on the stretcher in obvious pain and distress. He told Erin he was there and that everything would be ok. Her parents would be at the hospital when she arrived. He ran to the second ambulance and opened the door. Lindsay, looking up from the stretcher, saw him and was able to shout that she was ok, just as police removed him from the ambulance. He explained that he was Lindsay's father and was frantic for information. From the perspective of the police, however, Jeff was a stranger who had entered a crime scene investigation. He was less than welcome and was asked to leave the scene immediately.

Harborview Medical Center is the only level one trauma center serving Washington, Alaska, Montana and Idaho. The medical center offers highly specialized services, and as a rule receives all gunshot wounds. As we entered the emergency department, the lobby was filled. Homeless people had taken shelter there. Sick, listless children were being comforted by worried parents. Angry people wanting to see a family member that was being treated.

Erin's family met us there and the triage nurse immediately took us all back to see our girls.

As we walked through the doors it was like entering another world. People on stretchers lined the hallways. Doctors and nurses were scurrying about and there was a heavy police presence. I could see Lindsay on a stretcher in one of the exam rooms and I started crying once again. Lindsay saw us and shouted, "It's OK mom. I'm ok and it really doesn't hurt that bad." Lindsay is a people pleaser with a compassionate heart and a distaste for causing others distress. She is ever the trooper. The room was stark and medical debris and wrappers were strewn about. Gracing either side of the door were two police investigators, who introduced themselves and continued asking questions and taking photographs.

It dawned on me that I didn't even know where she'd been shot. The detectives pulled back the sheet covering her legs to show one of two angry, burned and dripping holes in her left leg. One bullet had entered her outer thigh just above the knee and exited out her inner thigh. There was a large bruise on her inner right thigh where the bullet had hit as it exited the left leg. The second bullet had entered her left leg at mid-calf and remained lodged in the deep tissue. The bullet had passed through the car door, a stack of 15 CDs stored in the door pocket, and her jeans. Doctors were concerned about the potential for infection and were trying to determine whether it would do more damage to remove the bullet or leave it in her leg. Jeff and I absolutely couldn't conceive of leaving the bullet in her body and voiced our concern. However, we didn't want surgery to potentially cause further damage to her leg. After consulting the surgeon and giving it much consideration, it was decided that with the trauma already put upon the leg and foot, it would be far worse to remove the bullet that would almost certainly encapsulate with scar tissue and cause no further damage.

Once Lindsay was stabilized, we went to check on Erin in another room. She had sustained injuries to both wrists from shrapnel passing through the door. Some pieces were, and remain to this day, lodged in her arm. One of the boys in the car was experiencing some back pain and bruising. Further trajectory investigation of the car revealed that the third bullet had passed through the car and into the back of the passenger seat. The only thing between his spine and the bullet was his shirt and the Hawaiian print seat cover. The other rear passenger didn't sustain any injuries. It was an absolute miracle that nobody was killed.

Later into the night, things began to unravel and go from bad to worse. Jeff, exhausted and emotionally spent, took Brittany home and planned to return in the morning. I stayed with Lindsay in the ER during the night.

Sometime early in the morning, Lindsay's sweet disposition turned sour and the reality of what had happened kicked in. Initially, she experienced mild pain in her leg and little to no feeling in her foot. The bullets had not hit any bones or major arteries, which was a blessing. Now, several hours into this nightmare, the adrenaline began to wear off and she was having severe leg pain with no feeling in her foot. The hospital was overflowing, and we were moved to a room that housed other patients, several of them delusional and shrieking throughout the night. I had spoken to my mom earlier in the evening to let her know Lindsay was alright and she mentioned that there was a story on the news about the shooting.

At that point, we were still in the dark as to any of the details surrounding the event. Lindsay said there was a caravan of three cars of friends heading to Dick's, a burger joint in Seattle. She recalls someone trying to pull over into her lane as they entered the freeway. She felt she was in their blind spot and thought they might hit her. Rather than slowing to let them over, she sped up, which resulted in cutting them off. About a mile or so up the road, the shooter fell back into place in the lane beside her. The front passenger in Lindsay's car looked over and said, "I think they have a gun!" The next thing Lindsay remembers is a series of loud noises and everything beginning to move in slow motion. She was aware of an "electrical" feeling coursing through her body and recalls Erin screaming in the back seat but didn't comprehend what had happened. She took her foot off the gas and the car started to slow down in the middle of the freeway. Realizing this could result in an accident for them or someone else, Pat told her to step on the gas as he turned the steering wheel to move onto the shoulder.

Once parked, Erin, bleeding heavily from her arms and quickly going into shock, got out of the car and laid down on a grassy hill, just above the shoulder of the roadway. Friends, who had been caravanning behind Lindsay and had seen what happened pulled over and began taking off shirts to cover Erin's arms. Pat ran around the car to look at Lindsay's leg and confirmed she'd been shot not once, but twice!

Several weeks prior to this, the family had been watching a show in which parents received a late-night call that showed on caller ID as being from a hospital. Jeff and I commented how scary that would be for any parent. Lindsay, during all the roadside confusion, remembered this and had the presence of mind to call us so we wouldn't panic when our own caller ID showed "Harborview Medical Center."

As my mom had indicated in our earlier conversation, the media had become involved in the investigation and had leaked both girls' names, age and city of residence to the public. We were furious. Police were still trying to determine whether the shooter had gang ties or could be a continued risk to the girls. Now, everyone knew their names and where they resided. During the night, we overheard a patient on the other side of the curtained partition talking on her cell phone. "One of the girls in the drive-by shooting last night is right next to me. Yes, really." It took everything I had not to whip the curtain aside and respond "Yes, and she can hear everything you're saying!" I'm not sure what the big story was. At the time, drive-by shootings weren't as commonplace as they are today. The fact that it happened in a highly populated area at 9pm on a Sunday evening added some interest, I guess.

Suffice it to say, it was an extremely long night. Lindsay was in pain despite being medicated, and neither of us had gotten any sleep. Since no surgery was needed for either of the girls, they were due for discharge later that day and I was given a crash course in bullet wound care. This was way beyond the standard bloody nose, bee sting or skinned knee event I was used to as a mom. We were both totally stressed out and sweating by the time I got her irrigated and appropriately bandaged up again.

Next on the agenda was a visit from the PT (personal terrorist?) from Hell, who had the worst bedside manner of any healthcare professional I've ever encountered. He walked in, introduced himself and briskly told Lindsay to sit up on the side of the bed. She had been flat on her back since arrival and was stiff and hurting. She sat up and very slowly began to scoot to the edge of the bed. She apologized for being so slow, to which he replied "You'll be fine. Take these crutches and do a lap around the outside hallway." Lightheaded she began hobbling toward the door, stopped to readjust the crutches and catch her breath. "You're fine, c'mon keep moving." I could see she was embarrassed, and I said, "She's just feeling overwhelmed right now, let's give her a minute." After a snort and exaggerated eye roll, he began walking alongside her, criticizing her every move and not uttering a single positive word. I noticed she was beginning to perspire heavily and choke back tears. I wanted to beat that bastard senseless with his damn crutches and criticism.

Lindsay managed to turn around and get back to her room where she sat on the side of the bed and proceeded to have the first panic attack of many that would follow her into adulthood.

So, shortly thereafter, we left the hospital in a wheelchair, with the fucking crutches in tow, one bloody flip-flop (the other was kept for evidence) and the biggest vial of pain medication I've ever seen. I began to channel my inner Sean Penn when I realized we were being photographed by news stations through the parking garage foliage. Sure enough, the girls appeared on the news that evening. Furious at the lack of respect for our privacy, we declined every interview request, left media phone messages unreturned and after about two weeks, the story began to fade away.

Walking into the house I was met by the climbing gear that had been dropped inside the door the day before. Talk about being in the right place at the right time! Had the weather permitted me to continue the climb, we would all still be on Mt. Rainier, instead of home when Lindsay was shot. We wouldn't have gotten word for hours and, even then, driving at the speed of light from Rainier to Seattle would have been dangerous for us all. That storm was divine intervention and I was thankful that things had worked out as they did.

Let the healing begin!

Recovery

Much of Lindsay's recovery is a blur for me. I realize now that I was recovering from the shooting as well. Recovering from the fact that my daughter had been the victim of a random, violent crime. Recovering from the realization that there is no safe place from someone who wants to do harm.

I recall returning to work for the first time after the shooting. I walked into my cubicle and after my friends and coworkers asked about Lindsay, they handed me a large manila envelope. "We made these to decorate your cubicle for the climb, but when we heard what had happened to Lindsay, we took them down. It didn't seem appropriate to celebrate anything." I opened the envelope and pulled out a huge stack of large hand-cut snowflakes from everyone at work who had contributed to my fundraising effort. I was really touched by the thought and time that had been put into such a nice surprise. I still have those snowflakes.

Lindsay has always had a large circle of close friends. Most of them met during elementary school and some have remained close since those early days. During the next few weeks, our house was full to overflowing with kids. At any given time, Lindsay's bedroom had four or five kids laying on the bed watching movies with her or talking to each other while she slept. There were flowers and treat baskets on every shelf. We received so much support during that time!

Since her mobility was severely restricted, Lindsay was homebound most of the time. I was concerned about her becoming dependent upon the pain medication and kept tight control over the dosing. In hindsight, I'm sure I made her wait longer than necessary for another round of meds. I decided to take some time off work to spend with her during her recovery and since it was summer, Brittany was home as well.

Despite my best efforts, Lindsay's lower leg where the bullet remained began to look suspicious. Less pink and more gray-green. Oozing a bit more. A bit of humor occurred when, on a Friday afternoon, concerned that we were heading into the weekend with a potential infection, I made an appointment to see our wonderful general practitioner. She was out of the office for the day so another doc at the clinic worked us in. It is important to remember that Edmonds is a small town with a relatively low crime rate. Certainly, gunshot wounds are not seen with great regularity at the local family practice. We explained the situation to the doctor and confirmed that we had been following instructions to the letter, but it appeared the wound had become infected.

The doctor took the dressing off the wound on Lindsay's thigh and seemed satisfied with the level of healing. She then removed the bandage from the wound on Lindsay's lower calf. She was silent as she investigated the leg. She paced back and forth for a few moments, wringing her hands and said, "The wound is definitely infected. I haven't seen anything like this since my days as a resident. Is it getting hot in here? I feel so warm suddenly. If you don't mind, I'm going to call my husband who happens to be an army trauma physician. We'll just waive your privacy rights, ok?" What I find humorous about this situation is that the shooting had been such a difficult situation for our family to wrap our heads around. It was a tremendous, life changing event for Lindsay and for us as a family. It was somehow reassuring to see an unjaded medical professional that was obviously affected by what she was seeing. Her nervous reaction was confirmation in my mind that we weren't over-reacting, that this was indeed a very big deal.

So, the following week we found ourselves back at Harborview for the removal of the bullet from Lindsay's seriously infected lower left leg. Yes, the same bullet we requested be removed the night of her arrival in the ER just weeks earlier. At age 18 this would be Lindsay's first surgery and we were all nervous about the outcome and potential damage. Jeff and Brittany were in the surgical waiting room and I was waiting while the team got the initial surgery prep in order to go back with Lindsay. They finally came to get me and explained that she didn't seem to be responding to the IV medication to make her drowsy prior to going to the OR and she was beginning to get anxious. They allowed me in the room to sit with her while they continued to increase the dosage of her IV cocktail.

Finally, she responded to the meds. With a vengeance! She started talking at warp speed. And didn't stop. She spoke to everyone assisting her, everyone walking by the door and everyone that looked like they MIGHT walk by the door. There was no shutting her up. The professionals were laughing and engaging her in conversation, teasing her and she was obviously feeling quite relaxed. As they wheeled her out in her neon green terry-cloth sweats and hot pink tee shirt that had "Hi, Mom!" emblazoned across the front, I heard her say "Hey, can I get some of this stuff to go? Woohoo!"

The surgery took about an hour and she came through very well. The infected tissue inside the wound had been removed and flushed, the burned skin had been debrided and circulation around the wound had increased and there was no more gray green color! Post procedure scans showed that the bullet had actually traveled to a different location in the lower front part of her leg than they originally thought. You could see a 5 inch "tunnel" burrowed down the front of her leg where the bullet had moved. Tight accordion-fold gauze was packed into the tunnel, her leg was wrapped, and we were sent on our way.

It was a huge relief to know that the surgery was a success and that her leg hadn't sustained any permanent damage. I looked at Jeff gazing lovingly at his dozing daughter in the back seat of the car. I was sure he was about to utter something warm and loving about his neon-clad baby girl. Smiling softly, he looked at me and asked, "Did we actually PURCHASE that hideous outfit she's wearing?"

Throughout Lindsay's recuperation, we were also involved in the police investigation and related auto and medical insurance red tape. Jeff was in contact with the investigators several times each day to check on the progress. Information was still sketchy and was kept close to the vest until they finally caught the shooter. Suffice it to say, he was a troubled young teen with an extensive criminal background. He and his friends were running drugs up and down the I-5 corridor when they encountered Lindsay and her friends. To share the details of the investigation, subsequent legal proceedings and insurance issues that continued throughout the next three years would require far more time and energy than I have. In many ways, having to deal with the loopholes in the "judicial system" and "due process" only adds insult to injury from the victim's viewpoint. Not only did she suffer a senseless, potentially fatal event, but the scope and duration of Lindsay's recovery and physical therapy altered the course of her future. She lost her vehicle to evidence impound and we were responsible for paying significant fees to release the car for auction. When Lindsay and Erin finally had their day in court nearly two years later, the defendant copped an Alford Plea, which means there is more than enough evidence for a guilty charge by the jury. Pleading guilty to a lesser charge means that the shooter received a sentence of house arrest, where he could still drive and attend school, hang out with friends, play video games, cut the ankle monitor off, punch out a cop and still be granted time served with "good behavior". He ended up walking out of the courthouse in front of us a free "man."

For my own sanity I had to forgive him. I asked if I could approach him and he nodded while eyeing me suspiciously. I looked at this handsome young man and asked him to please continue the path of "good behavior." I told him I forgave him for the pain his actions had caused my daughter and that I wished him well with his future. He nodded and walked on.

Lindsay's friends continued to visit her frequently and her wounds were healing well. She was unable to bear weight on her left leg and still had significant loss of feeling in her foot and she began physical therapy several times a week. During the day, the three of us had settled into a nice pattern of being home together, talking, watching movies and keeping that leg clean and germ free. Overall, things felt lighter and would be returning to normal soon.

One of the most difficult moments I remember during this period was when it came time to remove the accordion packing from the surgical site. We cleaned and soaked her leg in an attempt to soften the gauze tucked inside the tunnel. Lindsay sat on the bed and began to gently pull on the gauze. It didn't budge and obviously hurt terribly. I decided to try pulling the proverbial bandage off quickly and as Jeff crouched beside her on the bed, I gave a little tug. Still, no progress but shrieks of protest from Lindsay. She was crying and trying not to vomit from the pain. She decided she had to do it herself. My mom, Jeff and I were all dripping with sweat and near tears by the time she finished. About thirty minutes after we'd started, Lindsay removed the last of the 18 inches of packing. I had no idea that much packing was inside her leg! She flopped back on the bed, sobbing, as we all cheered and hugged her.

Jeff, pale, perspiring, and visibly upset, gave her a hug and a "good job, kiddo" and quickly left the room.

The Gift of Time

During the three weeks that I'd been home with the girls during the day, Jeff would come home from work, make dinner for the family and keep Lindsay occupied during the evening while Brittany and I would take a break to get out of the house for a walk, movie or trip to the mall. It was a welcome break and the perfect opportunity for Lindsay and Jeff to reconnect. They had always been very close, but the one-on-one time reading, talking, and watching movies benefited them both. It did my heart good to come home and find them together laughing over something they'd just watched. I believe "Dogma" and "Sean of the Dead" were two of their favorites. Hey, I never claimed they were watching anything educational!

I remember being annoyed with my dear lifelong friend one afternoon. She had stopped by to visit Lindsay and when I walked her to her car she said, "Is Jeff OK? He doesn't look well." I don't recall how I responded but I remember thinking that she just didn't get it! His daughter was the victim of a horrible violent crime. It takes a toll. He looked great to me.

By the end of July, I had returned to work full time. Living next door, my mom had been able to check on Lindsay periodically during the day. Brittany was home and friends still filled the house daily. With frequent physical therapy, Lindsay was slowly regaining the use of her leg, although still experiencing nerve damage in her foot. I voiced my concern about the ongoing use of the pain meds at a visit to the doctor. She agreed that it was time to make a switch from the Oxycodone to Neurontin, a drug used to treat epilepsy with promising results for nerve damage and pain. We would gradually begin weaning Lindsay off the narcotic and onto the therapeutic.

Things in our world were slowly beginning to right themselves and the initial stress and worry spurred by the shooting was beginning to dissipate. We were moving on!

And then, an interesting thing began to happen. Jeff and I started having deep, meaningful conversations about love, religion, life, and gratitude and wondered together about death and dying. We talked about our future together in a way we hadn't before. We were a young family and until this accident with Lindsay, never gave much thought to death or dying. We were so blessed that Lindsay was doing well and expected to make a full recovery and that, as horrific as the incident had been, nobody had been killed.

I was beginning to see just how profoundly the shooting had affected Jeff. He had always been a "man's man", strong, stoic and quiet. Of course, the kids and I knew he had a soft side and great sense of humor, but he didn't show that side to many people. I was seeing a softening around the edges that I had always known was there. It was a maturing of sorts that I think comes when your life is rocked to the core.

Goodbyes

The morning of August 3, 2005, Jeff and I chatted over coffee before heading off to work. As was our usual routine, we followed each other to my work exit and waved as he continued. He called me around 3:00pm and we talked about the day and our plans for the evening. It was a hot day and we would stay home tonight. Jeff would make tacos for dinner and I would complete a piece of jewelry I was making for a co-worker's birthday.

When we got home, Lindsay had gotten an invitation to watch movies with friends after dinner. This would be her first real outing since the shooting, and she was eager to see Erin and the others. Jeff and I talked while he made dinner and I enjoyed sitting at the table surrounded by jewelry makings. Brittany was popping in and out visiting with us. We were encouraged that Lindsay had the opportunity to be out of the house with friends. Things were calm. It was a nice evening.

And then, it wasn't.

After dinner, I went across the driveway to mom's house to return something I had borrowed. She and I visited for a few minutes while we watched Jeff take the garbage dumpsters down the driveway to the street for pick up the next morning. He returned, went into the house and I said goodbye to mom and headed back over.

As I entered the house, Jeff was walking over the threshold between the dining and living rooms. He turned to look at me when I walked in. Then he sighed, fell backward to the floor, hitting his head against the dining room chair and sending it across the room. For a brief second, I didn't realize what was happening and thought maybe he had tripped over something or passed out but, as I ran to him, I instinctively knew it was something far more serious. I don't remember some of what happened during those initial moments, but it was as if a switch was flipped. I remember complete chaos breaking loose in my brain. I began to cry and shriek and babble out of control.

Brittany, hearing Jeff fall and me screaming his name, came running out and stood paralyzed at her dad's feet. He lay on his back, looking around in a dazed manner and holding his hands up to his face as if to examine them. I tried to speak to him, but he was obviously not hearing or comprehending anything I was saying. I instructed Brittany to close the house as we'd probably need to go to the hospital.

I could hear that he was having trouble breathing and wasn't sure if there was something lodged in his throat. I wondered if he might vomit and tried to roll him over to avoid aspiration, but he was too heavy. I called 911 and as I was informing the operator that Jeff was having some sort of seizure, I listened to his breathing again and realized only stillness. No movement of air, no sound. I told the dispatcher I might be wrong and it maybe he'd had a heart attack! I immediately began CPR. The dispatcher worked with me and stayed on the line, assuring me help was on the way. At some point, mom came over and took over CPR while I ran down the long driveway to flag the aid car, which seemed to be taking an eternity. I can still recall looking over my shoulder as I ran out the door and witnessing my precious mom trying so desperately to save my husband.

Without question, those were the longest, most agonizing four minutes I have ever spent on this earth.

Three EMTs and one Incident Commander from Station 16 entered the house, shoved the kitchen table out of the way, which sent beads, tools and wire everywhere, cut off Jeff's shorts and favorite t-shirt and worked on him for 45 minutes right there on the kitchen floor. Mom, Brittany and I watched as they vigorously took over CPR, intubated him, gave injections and administered numerous electrical shocks. I could see his feet jump every time they shocked him and see the rhythm of the machines bounce and dance. Not once during this time did it occur to me that he would not survive. Not. Once.

Brittany had called Lindsay at her friend's house to tell her that something had happened to dad. It might be a heart attack and they're still working on him. Erin drove Lindsay home, but the ambulances and other emergency vehicles had blocked the drive and Lindsay wasn't able to walk up the drive with those fucking crutches. She and Erin opted to stay down on the street in the car where they could easily follow the ambulance when it took Jeff to the hospital for recovery.

I was in the bedroom on the phone with Jeff's dad and then his brother, waiting to tell him what hospital we'd be going to, when the Commander came in to tell me it was time to stop the effort and the Chaplain was on the way. I didn't want the Chaplain to come because he would likely talk to me about God, say things like "there's a reason this happened," or "he's in a better place." Well, screw that. I wanted Jeff here, where he belonged. Because life without him wasn't an option for us.

I immediately dissolved into an inconsolable, shaking mess of tears, spit, snot, shock and despair. I wanted nothing more than to pull it together to be available to console my girls but just couldn't make sense of the utter disbelief and chaos in my head. I was worthless to all and wandered around repeating "What am I going to do? What am I going to do?" Thankfully, family and friends immediately came to our side to help us through this nightmare.

Because Jeff was just three weeks shy of 42, his death was completely unexpected and happened outside of a medical facility, the Snohomish County Medical Examiner was called in to remove his body and conduct an autopsy to determine the cause of death. I immediately protested. What could be more brutal? I couldn't bear that thought. But the laws dictate otherwise, and I didn't have a choice in the matter. We were told it was a "busy night" and could be an hour or two before the ME would arrive to officially pronounce Jeff's death. In the meantime, he was to remain exactly as he lay, on the kitchen floor, clothes in shreds beside him, covered by a sheet. Family and friends were arriving, and I wasn't sure how to handle the situation. I didn't want everyone to have access to the visual in our kitchen, yet I didn't want to go next door to mom's house and leave Jeff "alone." I decided to uncover his face so he could "breathe" (remember, there's no crazy here!) and we routed family to mom's as they assembled. The Chaplain arrived, prayed with us and stayed quietly near to administer comfort and prayer as requested. Friends and family tried to offer comforting words, but I couldn't hear anything except the static bouncing around in my head. The first responders all spoke to me about how difficult it is to work a call such as ours, with someone so young and so loved. They called him by name and asked me questions about our life together. I appreciated that.

Finally, the white, windowless van made its way up the drive and the coroner entered our home. I greeted him, answered some questions, and then stumbled back over to mom's house. He said his exam would take a few minutes and he would let me know when I and others could return. A short time later, exam completed, official time of death recorded, we were told that if we wanted to see the body one final time, this was it. Let me tell you, my legs felt like lead as I made the long trek across the drive to say goodbye.

Jeff's youngest brother, Brittany and her dearest friend, and I slowly approached Jeff. His chest was purple and his veins protruding and angry looking. There was a cannula left in his upper arm and a vent tube in his mouth. As fearful as I was to acknowledge what had happened, I knew if I didn't look, really look, that I might forget something. Some fine detail. A freckle or scar. So, I looked at his hair, ears and sideburns, his blue eyes, long eyelashes and straight nose. His arms and hands.

I remember thinking that he would never know that I found an exact bracelet to replace the one we'd purchased together 15 years earlier that was still on his wrist. He'd never taken it off and it had a large crack down the center. He was worried that he'd lose it. I searched high and low and finally found one that I'd planned to give him at his birthday in three weeks. I'd been so excited to give it to him.

I stared at him until my eyes blurred. The coroner removed the bracelet and Jeff's wedding ring and handed them to me, along with a woven leather bracelet. He indicated that an autopsy would be performed at 8:30 a.m. the next morning. I asked him to "please be careful and gentle" and I walked out the door. There is something so terrible about being faced with the "last time." I knew once I left, I would never again see or feel his physical body again. The urge to turn and look over my shoulder was pulling me terribly, but I knew if I didn't walk out at that moment, someone would need to physically remove me. Lindsay observed through the window as they prepared to leave and then retreated to Jeff's side of our bed with the shredded yellow T-shirt. Brittany and I stood watching in the driveway as they placed my fine, strong, beautiful man, the better part of me, into the white windowless van and drove away. We watched until the taillights turned onto the main road and he was gone. Really, truly and forever. There are simply no words.

And then the thought popped into my head through the static. He knows. The conversations we'd recently had, the questions we had just asked ourselves and each other about heaven, and life after death. Now he knows.

All We Needed

Jeff and I met in 1982 when I was 17 and he was 19. He had already graduated high school, had a full-time job and was renting a house with a friend. He drove a 1964 Chevelle with an "oo-ooga" horn and seemed so much more mature than other boys I knew. I had heard from friends about what a great guy Jeff was and looked forward to meeting him at an upcoming party he was hosting. It was a packed house and when my friend pointed and said, "There's Jeff!" I turned to see a super cute guy, laughing and walking around with a cover to the arm of a chair on his head and tons of brown ringlets pouring out underneath. What a weirdo. It was love at first sight! I remember him being quiet, not in a standoffish way, but rather just taking things in around him. He had a hysterical, dry wit, a smile that could light up a room and the most beautiful blue eyes I'd ever seen. And an overabundance of curly brown hair. Wow, yes, that hair.

We started dating, became inseparable, and were married in February of 1985. We welcomed Lindsay into our family in 1987 and Brittany in 1989. We were blessed with a wonderful marriage that grew stronger as we grew older. He was my best friend, an excellent father to our children and a strong, protective partner. I knew I could count on him for help and support in any situation and he could always make me laugh. We shared common interests and had reached the point in our lives where we talked about what our lives would be like as empty nesters. We were planning for our future as a couple again and looked forward to traveling and spending quality time together.

I once asked him what his passion was. What made him tick. He responded, "As long as I'm with you and the girls, I'm happy. That's all I need." I felt the same way. We were a close loving family, and that was enough for us.

The Death Spot

The week following Jeff's death consisted of lots of wandering, crying, wringing of hands, excessive yawning and gasping for breath. We stayed at mom's house with family and the kids' friends coming and going, pouring through photographs and mementos, and planning Jeff's celebration of life. Many people stopped by to visit, leave gifts, cards and food. We were blessed to have so many people thinking of us and making sure we were being cared for. We had received so many flower deliveries that after filling the tables in the house, they filled the entire outside deck and stairs. It was heartwarming that there were so many tropical arrangements in keeping with Jeff's love of Maui. We hoped that they would last through a few more warm days so we could share them at the funeral service.

When we first returned to our house, it was a stifling evening and the air both inside and outside was completely still. As was becoming the norm, I was having a hard time breathing. When I entered the dining room, I noticed the hundreds of beads all over the floor and into the next room, where they stayed for another week or so. I did right the chair that had been tipped over when he fell, but that was about all I could muster. There was still medical waste and wrappers strewn about the floor. The first thing the girls and I did was to go to the laundry hamper and pull out all of Jeff's worn shirts and smell them. There was his familiar cologne and deodorant. Then we took his pillowcase and anything else we could find that smelled like him and put it into plastic bags to preserve his essence for as long as we could. We also decided to keep his yellow T-shirt, which had been cut off, discarded and now smelled slightly smoky from the many defibrillator shocks he had received. Lindsay slept with that garment fragment for quite some time.

Over time, I pretended not to notice that I was developing a phobia around the place on the floor where Jeff had laid that night. I would step over it, walk around it, avert my eyes, and even jump over it. One day I decided I needed to face my fear. What was my fear exactly? Who knows? Everything felt scary at that time. But this was my home and I needed to learn to make peace with that damn spot on the floor. I closed my blinds so nobody would see me and think me crazy. I stared at that spot for what seemed an eternity. I gingerly laid down exactly where Jeff had taken his last breath and waited for the floor to envelope me, or for me to burst into flames, or the sky to fall. Something! I truly expected some sort of reaction. The floor was cold and hard, as expected. Silence. I waited for the walls to begin shaking. But. Nothing. Happened. Well, that's not entirely true because lots of tears happened. I laid there sobbing and contorting for a long time until my makeup had run down the sides of my face and pooled in my ears. Then I got up, wiped my nose on my shirt and moved on. There was a strange sense of relief in the realization that the "death spot" only held as much power as I gave it. So, I took my power and my floor back.

The Send Off

The process of planning a funeral service for someone you love is both devastating and beautiful. I was fortunate to have mom, my brother and sister, their spouses and children to help with details and make decisions when my brain grew fuzzy and my eyes glazed over. Since his death was so unexpected, I encouraged the girls to write Jeff a letter, to express any personal thoughts they wanted to share with him. I did the same though I don't recall most of what I penned. My intent was to leave the letters at his gravesite. After thinking about it, I decided it would be more appropriate for him to have our final thoughts with him as he was cremated.

I tried to plan the service with two main goals in mind; to create something that Jeff wouldn't mind sitting through for someone else, and to make it my last loving gift to him. It was a heart-wrenching process but in the end, the service was wonderful. By "wonderful" I mean that it was well attended by family, coworkers and many, many friends. In keeping with Jeff's love of Maui, there were tropical flowers everywhere. The pastor, as well as family and many guests, wore Hawaiian inspired clothes. Mom shared later that she had never seen me look more beautiful or poised which, initially, I thought was a bit strange. Now, I think it is a wonderful compliment.

I remember joking with Jeff many years prior about who he thought would show up at his funeral? His response was "Nobody will show up to my funeral – I'm an ass!" How wrong he was. The chapel was overflowing with people who understood the magnitude of our loss. There was humor, laughter, tears and the sharing of stories. It was a wonderful tribute to a wonderful man.

As his brothers and I placed the urn containing Jeff's ashes into the ground, the true finality began to hit me. Guests began to leave, and I had an overwhelming urge to lie down on the grassy hill nearby and stare at the leaves moving above me. It was a muggy August day; I was exhausted, devastated and felt like I was suffocating. I wanted to feel that cool soft grass beneath me. Feel the solid earth holding me up. See the blue sky, color and movement. I was worried that any remaining guests might feel uncomfortable with my "unconventional" behavior or think I'd "lost it" but what did I care? Would I ever really care about anything again? My brother followed me to the hill and sat quietly with me while I hiked my dress up over my knees, kicked off my shoes and sprawled out on the lawn.

Autopsies & Dragonflies

About four weeks after Jeff's death, I received a call at work from the Medical Examiner's office telling me that the autopsy report was complete and ready to be collected at my convenience. I had received basic details surrounding the cause of death based on a phone conversation I'd had with the coroner a few days following the autopsy, yet I was starving for more information. I wanted to know exactly what had gone wrong in the beautiful body that I had so loved. I wanted details and explanations that would make it all clear to me. Answers.

The offices of the Snohomish County Medical Examiner are difficult to locate; off the beaten path for obvious reasons. The building sits amid wetlands, with a marsh and tall trees on the perimeter. There is a well-maintained greenbelt with flowers and benches. I'm not sure what I was expecting, but it wasn't this beautiful park-like setting. I walked into the building and entered a small, light-filled reception area. From there, I could see down a hallway of closed doors. The receptionist greeted me warmly and before I realized it, the gentleman that had been in my home only weeks prior, examining my husband on the kitchen floor, stepped around the corner. I would have recognized him anywhere, and as he shook my hand and handed me the envelope, I felt like I'd been sucker-punched. Those hands had explored Jeff's body more personally than I ever had and understood his death in a way I never would. I quickly thanked him and retreated to the car, where I laid the envelope on the passenger seat and stared at it.

I knew I should leave and read the report in the privacy of my home, but those critical answers were right there, riding shotgun. Taunting me.

I reached for the envelope, peered inside as if something might jump out, and removed the document. It was several pages in length, stapled in the upper left corner and contained descriptions and evidence of disease of major organs and body systems, and included toe and wrist tag numbers. It was clinical, sterile and matter of fact, apart from the first page, which consisted of a "visual" observation prior to the autopsy. Tears began to flow as I read the first page, which I found to be a beautiful physical description of the man I had loved. It spoke of clean short hair and tidy beard. Straight, white teeth, blue eyes and a clear complexion. Neatly trimmed finger and toenails and noted the four blue-green turtles tattooed on his right calf. The turtles were meant to symbolize our family and he had chosen them while on one of our cherished Maui vacations. I can still see the eye roll he gave me across the room that day when the first drop of ink penetrated his skin!

Jeff died of sudden cardiac arrest at 41 year of age. Perplexed by the damaged and enlarged condition of his heart, I had given the coroner permission to test the vitreous fluid in Jeff's eyes to see if his glucose levels were elevated. It came back at just under 1,000 mg/dl, which is astounding. Undiagnosed Type 2 diabetes was the underlying cause of Jeff's atherosclerotic buildup, resulting cardiac arrest and sudden death. I have two words for you. Fuck. Diabetes.

I believe signs are all around for us to see. Sometimes we are more tuned in to them and other times we are aware of them for a reason. At one point, I loved dragonflies and became an avid collector of anything that related to the magical insects and what they represent; change, living in the moment, and the opening of one's eyes. That afternoon at the Medical Examiner's office, as I sobbed in my car, I noticed a tapping sound. I looked up and there on the windshield wiper was a dragonfly. I watched it for several minutes as it fluttered in the warm August sunshine. Finally, when I felt collected enough to drive, I started the car and pulled out into late afternoon, congested traffic where I crept for about 40 minutes.

I decided to stop by the beach as I wasn't ready to go home yet. As I pulled up along the waterfront, I noticed that the dragonfly had accompanied me for the whole commute. It was still there, on the wiper as it had been earlier. A short while later, feeling calmer and ready to go home, I started the car and pulled away from the curb. The dragonfly fluttered one last time and flew off over the bluff. I felt it was a sign that Jeff had been here with me, stayed with me through the tough part and then, when I was ready to face the world again, he was off!

To my amazement, a similar sign presented itself just a few days later. My sister-in-law didn't want me to go alone to pick up the death certificates that I'd ordered. She suggested I pick her up on the way, drop the girls off to spend time with their cousins, and the two of us would go together. While downstairs chatting, my nephew called out, "Aunt Kelly, look in the backyard, quick!" We went to the window and there, in the back yard, was a swarm (do dragonflies swarm?) of at least fifty, flitting up and down and in circles. Everyone in the house that day can attest to seeing this! Again, I chose to believe it was a sign from Jeff. Sending me a bit of strength when I needed it the most.

Ashes and Apple Trees

Jeff died just three weeks before his 42nd birthday. Before his death, we had been discussed celebrating his birthday by having a Hawaiian themed barbecue. As the date grew nearer, I felt very strongly that it needed to be celebrated. I invited friends and family over and it was the perfect opportunity to get together, touch base on how we were all getting along and enjoy some quality family time.

A few days before the party, my sister and I placed a Hawaiian tapestry and family photographs on the table, played "Somewhere Over the Rainbow" by Iz, and transferred some of Jeff's ashes from the urn to a small, carved wooden box. Later, during the party, there were a few moments when the box was passed around to everyone to say a little something or just hold a quiet thought. Then, I placed the box under the apple tree in our backyard. The tree was a huge part of our family history in that my grandparents had planted it, I had eaten its fruit as a kid, and our girls had climbed the limbs and played beneath it. It was like a living, breathing part of the family. It was good to be around family, to laugh and cry, to support one another. I think everyone enjoyed the occasion and I was glad for the opportunity to focus on Jeff's birth, rather than his death. Celebrate how lucky we were to have shared our lives with him.

Circling the Drain

The months following Jeff's death and funeral were filled with tedious tasks and chores as we learned to navigate our new normal. Removing his name from this or that, changing or closing accounts, deciphering financial information, going through clothes and belongings.

Shortly after returning to my work in the biotech industry, I learned that our business operations would be moving across the country to Indianapolis. The company was being acquired by big pharma and would cease to exist. I, along with the remainder of the legal department, would be working on completing the acquisition, and working ourselves out of jobs. Everyone would be looking for work. Morale was very low. I recall walking with my boss through the hallway and someone said, "Look, it's Satan and his three-headed dog." I worked sporadically and was blessed to have caring, compassionate co-workers that allowed me whatever time, space, hugs or conversation I needed. My boss was abundantly patient and kind. I came and went, pretended to be focused when I was there, concealed crying spells in the restroom and allowed people to be kind to me.

My greatest concern was that I now "looked" like a widow. What does a widow look like exactly? I have no idea, but I was certain I had the mark. I didn't want people to pity me or treat me differently, yet I didn't want them to act as if nothing had happened either. What did I want then? I wanted to run screaming through the halls. I wanted to sink into the ground to the cool darkness below. I wanted to sit and stare at the wall without someone asking if I was ok. I wanted to break free of the gray fog that inhabited my brain and the cotton that filled my lungs. I wanted to stop sighing all the time. I wanted to smash things with a baseball bat. I wanted to stay in that peaceful, drowsy space between sleep and waking when I didn't yet remember what had happed. I wanted to laugh a huge gut busting laugh about how ridiculous and unfair the events of the last few months had been. I wanted to make things okay for my children. I wanted people to stop asking each other "how is she doing?" in hushed tones when I was standing in earshot.

I wanted my husband back. My life back. I would do anything. Anything.

I remember one afternoon shortly after the funeral, I sat down on the floor directly in front of a fan. The air was so refreshing yet I still couldn't take a deep breath. I just kept sighing. I couldn't breathe anymore! I didn't even know it was coming but I began to cry and then the floodgates opened. Oh, the pain. I rocked back and forth, sobbing in front of the fan until I was absolutely soaked and drained. Both my mom and Jeff's mom came to me and held me for a very long time. That was my moment of complete and total desperation. I have never felt worse and I hope never to revisit it. I remember briefly feeling that I too wanted to die. And that scared me. I was frightened by these thoughts, frightened by what would become of me. Become of my kids. Of our lives. How would we survive without this man? How would we make it out of this alive?

Wreckage

Lindsay has since confided that due to the shooting and investigation, and the doctor's recommendation to increase her medication the day before the funeral, she doesn't remember much, if anything of her father's funeral.

For a long time, she never had any type of closure. She saw her dad for dinner, she left the house for a night of fun, and she never saw him again. How did she know he hadn't just gone someplace? She saw them take a body out of the house, but it had been covered. She couldn't be sure it was really him. He might still walk in the door. She built barriers and refrained from discussing Jeff in any sort of meaningful way with Brittany or me and would avoid anything that might spark an emotional outburst at all costs. She once told me she didn't want to cry because if she started, she might never stop.

Oh, a mother's heart!

She began having major health issues and debilitating anxiety and was later diagnosed with Systemic Sclerosis, more commonly referred to as Scleroderma, a rare and life-threatening, autoimmune, and connective tissue disease.

Sclero-what?

Sclero means "hard" and derma means "skin." Scleroderma is an autoimmune disease affecting the skin and other organs of the body, meaning that the body's immune system is causing inflammation and other abnormalities in these tissues. The main finding in scleroderma is thickening and tightening of the skin and inflammation and scarring of many body parts, leading to problems in the lungs, kidneys, heart, intestinal system and other areas. There is still no cure for scleroderma but effective treatments for some forms of the disease are available. Scleroderma is relatively rare. About 75,000 to 100,000 people in the U.S. have this disease; most are women between the ages of 30 and 50. A great deal of research is also underway to find better treatments for and, hopefully, someday a cure.

Little Wing

For many months, people who saw Brittany ("Bird") would tell me that she looked like a deer in the headlights. Absolutely wide-eyed and petrified most of the time. Lost. Uncertain. Always a daddy's girl, she became my shadow after Jeff's death, not wanting to be alone for long.

After the shooting, she began struggling in school and, unbeknownst to me, was not attending much of the time. Thinking I could easily help rectify her absences by delivering her to campus, I took her to high school every morning and watched her walk into the back side of the building. As I drove off to work, it didn't occur to me that she was walking out the front door.

One afternoon, upon receiving an urgent call from the school counselor, I knew we were at a breaking point. Brittany had passed her junior year of high school but with about fifty forged excused absence notes under her belt was told she would not be able to graduate with her class as a senior. I pulled her out of school, she enrolled in the EdCap program at the local community college where she later received her GED and some assorted college credits.

A Type 1 diabetic from the age of 11 months old, the stress was taking a tremendous toll on her, both emotionally and physically, and noncompliance with her health needs became the norm. She escaped her emotional pain by sleeping excessively and struggled terribly with depression. She would later suffer several strokes and require two life-saving craniotomies.

What is Type 1 Diabetes

Type 1 diabetes (T1D) is an autoimmune disease in which insulin-producing beta cells in the pancreas are mistakenly destroyed by the body's immune system. T1D has a genetic component and can be diagnosed early in life but also in adulthood. Its causes are not fully known, and there is currently no cure. People with T1D are dependent on daily injected or continuously pumped insulin to survive.

Beyond Difficult

Among other things, both girls worried significantly that something terrible would happen to me and they would be left completely alone. They took to sleeping in my room with me at night; Lindsay sharing my bed and Brittany on a mattress on the floor. I couldn't help but feel we were all circling the drain in our own ways. Grasping at whatever we could find before going down.

It was beyond difficult.

After Words

What you don't realize as you're reading this chapter is that it's been quite a while since I sat down to write. Years, in fact. We are fast approaching the 14-year anniversary of events that led to our new normal. And life has indeed continued to move "forward" but never "on."

When I first embarked on this writing journey, I wanted to provide insight and concrete answers to people in the midst of despair, fear and grief; provide step-by-step guidance on how to "get over it" and "move on" with your life, as people had suggested I do. What a ridiculous concept! Forgive my audacity, I know better now. My new and improved goal is simply to finish the story to the extent that's possible. It's difficult to know how and where to conclude. If I've provided you a moment of peace, comfort, or a laugh along the way, my mission has been a success.

There are times when it truly seems an eternity has passed, and there are times when it seems like yesterday. The events of 2005 have helped to shape who I am and who my kids are. I am clueless how our coping mechanisms and healing processes work. Thankfully they do. The human spirit is full of hope and resilience. Damn if that isn't infuriating sometimes!

I'd like to share what I have learned along the way and believe with all my heart to be true. Please humor me.

Much to my dismay, the world did not fall from its axis when my husband died. Since that time, seasons have bloomed in full color and stormed in hues of gray I never knew existed. During the worst pain my heart continued to beat.

I remember some very wise and brave words that Jeff's great aunt shared with me once. We were at her husband's funeral and I was holding Lindsay, who was just ten days old. She took Lindsay in her arms and after several minutes said, "This is at it should be. An old soul leaves the earth and a new soul enters." We are brave. We are survivors, and we do the hard work of grieving because there's no way to avoid it. You must meet it head on like a downpour when your umbrella blows inside out.

I woke up every day, went to work, loved my kids, paid the bills, fed the dogs, kept appointments, bought groceries, muddled through the mundane and managed to find rays of light and moments of joy when I least expected it. If I could bottle the feeling of laughter through tears, I'd be retired on a tropical island, drink in hand. There is no better feeling.

I've screamed, cried, tripped, fallen, bargained and shaken my fists at the heavens. But at the end of the day, there is no other choice. Reality stares you in the face like a petulant child and triple- dog-dares you to do it again. So, you do. And it gets easier. Slowly but surely. Day by day. Sometimes minute by minute.

My promise is this. You will not always feel like you do right now. I used to get so mad when people would tell me that at first, but I'm telling you that now because, well, it's true. I remember when I first realized my grief had changed shape. I was running errands and stopped at an intersection in front of a funeral home. There had been a service recently and there were still guests milling about, hugging one another and dabbing at eyes and noses. I felt sad for them and what I knew they were feeling and experiencing. What new normal they would be discovering. And a wave of relief passed through me. I was so glad to no longer feel that raw, razor's edge of pain.

I know that I am an inherently positive person. After my own diagnosis of Type 1 Diabetes at the ripe old age of 50, the death of my beloved mom, and the grief associated with leaving and eventually selling my family home and the history within those walls and under that apple tree, I realize I'm still happy. Life is indeed good, and when it gets tough, I'm far too stubborn to go down without a fight. Tooth and fucking nail.

I know that you can apply the saying "Fake It 'til You Make It" to any situation. Put a smile on your face and work it. If you don't feel better, you'll look good trying and your smile might make someone else's day.

I know that our hearts want nothing more than to love and be loved…and that love can be as sweet as honey the next time around. I remarried in 2010 and it doesn't compete with or take a thing away from the memories I have of life and love with Jeff. Dating was terrifying and hive-inducing but, I trusted the process, trusted my gut (and the background check!) and am lucky to have found a wonderful man that has embraced my life and all that it entails.

I know that despite illness, brain surgeries, chemotherapy and all the frightening shit that has hit their proverbial fans, my beautiful daughters have thick skin, gentle hearts and are strong, resilient, kick-ass young women, with hearts of gold. I'd like to think the apple doesn't fall far from the tree.

I promise that you are here for a reason. You will survive, and maybe, just maybe, you will thrive! We owe it to those we've loved and lost to do our best to return to happiness. Say their names, tell their stories, keep their memories alive. They were here. They were and always will be loved. They matter.

There is life after loss. Live it. One step at a time.

Grief is a journey. It never ends, but it changes. It is a passage, not a place to live. It is not a sign of weakness, or a lack of faith. Grief is the price of love.

Jeff and I, 1982, Woolworth photo booth.

Jeff and the girls, 1992 at Ocean Shores, Washington.

Jeff, Lindsay and Brittany, 1997, Cannon Beach, Oregon

Brittany and Lindsay, 2003, Whidbey Island, Washington

Rainier, 2005 *(I'm on the far right and my sister Terri is in the middle.)*

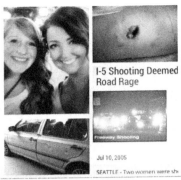

Shooting, 2005

Brittany and Lindsay, 2007, Maui, Hawaii

Lindsay, 2009

Brittany, 2009

Brad and me, 2014.

Brad, 2016

My loves, Thanksgiving 2016

Made in the USA
Middletown, DE
16 July 2019